Crowdfunding Personal Expenses

By Salvador Briggman

Copyright © 2016 Salvador Briggman LLC

All rights reserved. No part of this publication may be reproduced, distributed, or transmitted in any form or by any means, including photocopying, recording, or other electronic or mechanical methods, without the prior written permission of the publisher, except in the case of brief quotations embodied in critical reviews and certain other noncommercial uses permitted by copyright law

Although the author and publisher have made every effort to ensure that the information in this book was correct at press time, the author and publisher do not assume and hereby disclaim any liability to any party for any loss, damage, or disruption caused by errors or omissions, whether such errors or omissions result from negligence, accident, or any other cause.

The book is not intended for use as a source of legal or financial advice. You should always consult legal and financial professionals to provide specific guidance in evaluating and pursing investment or business opportunities. The advice, examples, and strategies in this book are not suitable for every situation. The materials are not intended to represent or guarantee desired results.

http://www.crowdcrux.com

Introduction

Yes, it's true, crowdfunding is a NEW way to help pay for personal expenses. These could include medical bills, emergency costs, and memorial funds. Crowdfunding can also be used to help pay for your education expenses or volunteer efforts. But, that's not all.

Crowdfunding isn't just for charity or personal cause campaigns. Believe it or not, more and more newlyweds are turning to crowdfunding to pay for their honeymoon! Some are even using it to pay for travel expenses!

I've been writing about crowdfunding since 2012 and have seen more campaigns than you can imagine. Last year alone, I helped nearly 400,000 individuals raise money from the crowd through my website, podcast, newsletter, and forum.

Even though crowdfunding is an amazing tool, there's a right and a wrong way to raise funds online. That's where I come in. I'm going to guide you through the murky waters and share with you the best techniques, strategies, and give you the inside scoop on some of the crowdfunding platforms and websites out there.

I'll also give you a heads up on costly MISTAKES TO AVOID when launching your first campaign. Believe me, you don't want to make a fool of yourself or learn the hard way. I'm going to make it dead simple and give you the step-by-step guide for raising money online. All you'll have to do is copy it!

-Sal

P.S. There is a FREE bonus video at the end of this ebook. I hope it's helpful!

Table of Contents

Chapter 1: Dispelling Myths 1
Chapter 2: Crowdfunding Platforms 7
Chapter 3: Creating a Great Campaign 17
Chapter 4: Outreach Mistakes (What not to do) 25
Chapter 5: Marketing Your Campaign 30
Chapter 6: Alternatives to Personal Fundraising 54
Chapter 7: Conclusion 61

Chapter 1: Dispelling Myths

Personal crowdfunding platforms have been around for several years. They've proven to be a great way to raise money for just about anything, like emergencies, charities, memorials, and events. But, you can't just blindly launch a project, cross your fingers, and hope that you meet your fundraising goal. Unfortunately, the media has given us a distorted image of these campaigns, which just sets many up to be unprepared and fail to raise funds.

I don't want that to happen to you, which is why this chapter will dispel some common myths about personal crowdfunding. Setting realistic expectations is the first step to coming up with a great plan for your fundraising campaign.

Myth #1: There are people on the Internet just waiting to give you money

Even though this would be nice, it isn't true. There are backers who do support rewards-based crowdfunding campaigns on platforms like Kickstarter and Indiegogo, but the majority of personal crowdfunding campaigns raise money from the first and second degree connections of the campaigner. Donors won't just fall into your lap.

You might have this perception because there have been some extremely popular personal crowdfunding campaigns that have blown up in the media. These are the outliers, not the norm. Typically, these campaigns have some kind of story or underlying message that appeals to a broad audience. The story was picked up by a social bookmarking website, like Reddit, or a major media publication, and went viral.

For example, a personal fundraising campaign for a Boston homeless man named Glen James quickly took off after he turned in a backpack that contained over $40,000 in cash and travelers checks in September of 2013. He was heralded as an honest man and a GoFundMe campaign that was launched in his honor raised $160,252 from 6,490 people in 31 months.

As another example, in April of 2013, a GoFundMe campaign was launched for Jeff Bauman who suffered severe injuries as a victim of the Boston Marathon Bombing incident. His friends launched this personal crowdfunding campaign to help pay for Jeff's medical bills. It raised $810,000 from 16,520 in 36 months.

Finally, The Chive and a Sister's Love helped raise $400,000 for a young woman who "faced the unthinkable." After beating cancer twice, this young woman was left paralyzed and imprisoned in an inaccessible apartment that she couldn't afford to move out of. Unable to watch her sister suffer any further, Stephanie Smith launched an online fundraising campaign and beseeched Chive Charities, a group that encourages its community to support orphan causes, to take on her case in March. Moved by Stephanie's love for her sibling and Smith's survival spirit, the CHIVEFund decided to donate $50,000 to Smith and urged others to do the same.

Once Chive Charities publicized Smith's story, her struggle went viral and the donations started pouring. At one point, Smith calculated that she was getting $837 per minute, she told WBAL-TV. To date, donors have pledged nearly $400,000, breaking Chive's previous fundraising record.

Myth #2: It doesn't matter what your crowdfunding page looks like

This is one of the biggest reasons that personal crowdfunding campaigns receive so few donations. Often times, the creator of a fundraising campaign thinks that just because their cause is genuine and they are in-need that others out there in the universe will recognize this and judge their campaign on these merits.

With so many scammy crowdfunding campaigns in the news recently, it's more important than ever to invest time in putting together a great campaign page that includes your story, high quality images, correct spelling, and possibly a video (though not necessary). You don't want to come off as untrustworthy or like you're just mooching off society in some way. As we'll cover in chapter 3, you're also going to be sharing the campaign page on your own social network, so you want to put some thought into it!

Your campaign page doesn't have to be as flashy and professional-looking as we expect with crowdfunding campaigns on sites like Kickstarter and Indiegogo, but it should include photos, a compelling description, and a title that stands out. If your page looks like a mess, it will be very hard to hold people's attention long enough for them to read your story or donate to your cause.

Myth #3: You need thousands of friends to raise money

The truth is that very few personal crowdfunding campaigns go viral and attract the attention of thousands of complete strangers. The best strategy is to focus on your immediate connections, people you know, and work your way up from there. Chances are that any strangers who support your project will be friends of friends. Don't have a big social network? Don't worry.

Take some time before launching your campaign to reconnect with old friends and acquaintances, and even make new friends! This is the time to add value to other people's lives before asking for something in return. I don't think it's a good idea to seek "give and take" relationships, but your friends or your local community will certainly be more likely to donate to your crowdfunding campaign if you've added tremendous value to their lives.

Myth #4: Platforms will promote your project for you

When choosing a personal crowdfunding platform, keep in mind that they are not going to do all of the work for you. If a platform claims that just posting your project on their site will get you the exposure you need, don't believe them. Even though some platforms feature projects on their front page, creators have to drive traffic to their own campaign first.

You need to be ready to bring the majority of the donations to your campaign. Platforms aren't going to promote a project that can't get donations on its own. If you're already seeing traction and donations, a platform might get involved to help you market your project, because it will also benefit their website. However, if you're not seeing traction, then the platform will be unlikely to do so.

Myth #5: All you need is a 'donate' button to raise thousands

You may be under the impression that a simple 'donate' button on your website or Facebook page is enough to raise money online, but it takes more than that. Having a dedicated fundraising page with a custom URL, short video (or relevant pictures), description of your cause, and simple donation interface will make a big difference. There is no magical, one-minute fundraising solution. Be ready to give it your full effort and you will be repaid with more donations.

On average, 75% of GoFundMe users set a goal of $1,000 or less and the average user raises $1,126. This is not the hundreds of thousands of dollars that the media leads us to believe. The most popular categories include: medical, education, volunteering, and emergency expenses.

Myth #6: All personal fundraising platforms are the same

Do you feel like all personal fundraising platforms are basically the same? That whichever one you choose, it won't really impact on your success? Actually, there are several things that you should consider before making a decision on which platform you will work with.

For example: How much will platform and transaction fees cost? Do they use fixed or flexible funding? (With flexible funding you get to keep the money you raised even if you don't reach a pre-set goal.) What is the procedure for withdrawing the funds you raise? How is the platform's customer service? What kinds of reviews does the platform get?

All of these should be taken into account and can absolutely effect how well your project does. We'll go over some of the differences between personal fundraising websites in the next chapter.

Myth #7: It's all about the money

For most creators of personal crowdfunding campaigns (especially when it comes to emergencies), money is pretty important. What many people don't focus on are the other benefits that can come from running a campaign, like gaining exposure for your cause and educating people about it (this can be especially important for non-profits). It's also a great opportunity to re-establish relationships and involve others in your mission or life. As I mentioned earlier, personal connections are important. The more people connecting to your story, the better for your campaign.

Personal crowdfunding campaigns can have a way of bringing people together that does good beyond a campaign's original purpose, so keep your eyes open for these opportunities.

Myth #8: You're going to seem like a beggar

In myth #3 I brought up the importance of social networks for personal fundraising projects. Many people are embarrassed to ask their friends and family for money online when they launch a personal fundraising campaign, and they worry that people will think badly of them. If you do it the wrong way, this might be true, but it doesn't have to be.

By making your "ask" personal, honest, and story-driven, you'll be able to touch the hearts of the people around you. By showing appreciation to the people who donate to your campaign, you'll encourage even more people to give. In chapter 4, we'll go over some outreach mistakes and in chapter 5 we'll talk about marketing your campaign.

Conclusion

As you can see, the media has certainly generated interest around personal crowdfunding or fundraising for personal expenses, but it has also spread a lot of myths that could misguide you about how online giving works. Challenging these assumptions is the first step to building a solid plan and achieving your goals.

Whatever you're thinking right now or whatever doubts you might have, I can guarantee you one thing. You can do this. This guide will give you all of the tools you need to plan and launch a successful fundraising campaign. If you choose a great platform and follow my easy steps, you'll be a pro in no time.

Chapter 2: Crowdfunding Platforms

In case you haven't already noticed, there are A LOT of personal crowdfunding platforms to choose from. I'm going to cover the top 8 in this chapter, but keep in mind, this list is not exhaustive. I'll go over how to pick the right one for your project and some of the aspects that set each of them apart, like fees and customer reviews.

#1: GoFundMe

You could argue that GoFundMe is one of the most recognized personal crowdfunding platforms. The platform launched in 2010, and has helped users raise over $1 billion in the past year! GoFundMe has no campaign deadlines or goal limits, and they advertise 5-minute customer support. GoFundMe takes a 5% fee from all donations and transaction fees vary from 1.4% - 4.25%. Even though most of this sounds good and GoFundMe campaigns seem to make it into a lot of media stories, the platform gets a lot of mediocre customer reviews. These including complaints about bad customer service, campaigns getting suspended for no reason, and users not being able to access the funds they raised.

One user reported on Highya.com, "A GoFundMe was set up for our grandson for college after the death of our daughter. A donation was made and subsequently transferred into our account after the required "waiting period". 28 days later they removed the funds without any warning. We have tried no less than 15 times to contact the company even with the organizers permission and NO explanation."

Another user left a bad review on BestCompany saying, "Terrible terrible my friend and her fiancé past away last December leaving two boys orphaned so we started a gofundme page as a trust account and we still haven't received funds we raised. 18 months later!! Fighting back and forth only by email for them to do a complete circle of request we complete then the sign a new person to email us to start again. Terrible no contact number or physical address. Garbage site!!!!"

These negative reviews might steer you away from GoFundMe, but it's important to keep in mind that there are also many many happy users that have successfully raised money for their personal expenses on the website.

The GoFundMe website features a long list of success stories, including the Jake Brewer memorial education fund, which raised over $424K from more than 5,000 people in just 15 days. Another campaign, Save the Abandoned Chimps, raised more than $218K from 4,000 people over a period of four months.

Several users have left positive reviews of the platform on other websites. One poster shared on CrowdsUnite, "We have been pleased with the results of our campaign on GoFundMe, both in terms of dollars raised and number of donors. The page is very attractive, allowing you to incorporate video, copy, photos, and graphics, giving donors the chance to comment, and easily allowing visitors to share the page through various social media channels. It also takes a minimum away for overhead, resulting in more funds for our cause."

#2: YouCaring

Founded in 2011, YouCaring has helped users raise over $335 million, with daily access to funds, real-time customer support, quick setup, and mobile optimization. The website says there are no platform fees to use YouCaring, only credit card processing fees (typically 2.9% + $.30 per transaction). However, your donors will be asked to provide a donation to the platform upon checkout.

Customer reviews for YouCaring are mainly positive. Customers find the platform easy to use, with responsive customer service. Some customers have had issues with payment processing (but most users say that can be fixed by switching from PayPal to WePay).

A lot of the campaigns featured on YouCaring are personal ones asking for help with things like paying medical expenses for a family member or sick pet. Others have to do with memorials or celebrations (like a wedding). One recent campaign has raised over $645K to save a Canadian man with Leukemia. YouCaring has seen its share of scammers, with a duplicate account set up to raise money for Alan Barnes, a disabled pensioner who was mugged outside his home last month.

One user left a negative review on Pissedconsumer.com saying, "I had a very negative experience with YouCaring. A friend of mine had started a fundraiser to help her dog rescue. A few days into the fundraiser, YouCaring shut it down. Weeks later I found out through [Facebook] that the shelter never received any donations ... I finally got a refund but no apology or explanation for their terrible business practices ... If you shut down a fundraiser you should immediately notify donors and offer them a prompt refund. Aside from the obvious actions they should have taken, they should have addressed my inquiries and apologized for their sloppy response time."

Another user left a positive review on the same website sharing, "Setting up the donation page was very easy and intuitive. Adding offline donations has been a great feature, as many people have been donating cash or cheque, and we want to include them in our list of supporters. Adding updates for our supporters to read up on our story has been a great feature to the site as well. We love that 100% of the donation goes to us, other than the percentage PayPal takes. Overall, we have had a very positive view of YouCaring."

As with all crowdfunding websites, there will be happy and not so happy customers. Personally, I think that the newly updated design/user interface of YouCaring is more attractive than GoFundMe, but GoFundMe certainly has more clout in the personal fundraising space.

#3: DepositaGift

It might surprise anyone familiar with crowdfunding and online fundraising that I'm including DepositaGift as number three on my list, but I wanted to highlight them due to their high degree of customer service and personalized attention. Although they are not as large as some of the other websites in this list, they have proven over time to be a consistent thought leader for my own community. I have done two personal fundraising webinars with this platform and each time they've been thorough in providing great information for the audience and answering questions. By the way, I am in no way being paid to include them in this ebook as #3 in our list.

DepositaGift launched in 2010 and customers like them for their easy setup, responsive customer service, low fees, and flexible fund withdrawal. DepositaGift offers three plans ranging from 2% - 4% and a credit card fee of 3.5%. They also have features that you can't find anywhere else – like the ability to sell event tickets. With DepositaGift, you keep all of your donations even if you don't reach your goal and you get to decide when to withdraw funds, which are sent to you for free via ACH's safe direct deposit.

Overall, there are a lot of happy customers, like this one who left a review on TrustPilot saying, "We did our first crowdfunding event and it worked great. The website was easy to use. They were very helpful and answered all my questions." Another reads, "Depositagift.com and their team was an absolute pleasure to work with. They surprised us with the high level of hands-on support, giving us not only a platform that was easy to use but also the tools to ensure us success."

I have found a few negative reviews of DepositAGift, but I think that the pros outweigh the cons. One review on TrustPilot reads, "The fees are not clearly stated up front. Also, the process of cashing out was a challenge. There has to be an easier way to complete transactions. Having to wait for a representative to contact you and then get approval from the manager. The family that we were donating to are still waiting for the check to come. This week makes almost two weeks of waiting."

Another review on TrustPilot underlines the need to update the user interface saying, "It's a good service and I would use it again. I wish the pages could be customizable to look nicer. The available graphics are chunky and you can't upload custom graphics." This was reiterated by another user, saying "Update your design options! The web "customization" is fine, but the graphic options are way out of date and make the final web pages look really stale and old school."

Despite some of the shortcomings, I've always had a great collaborative experience with the website and have only heard good things from readers that have used it.

#4: GiveForward

GiveForward launched in 2008, and has since helped users raise over $185 million for a range of causes. When it comes to fees, GiveForward does things a little bit differently. There is a 2.9% + 30 cent transaction fee and a 5% platform fee, but donors have the option to pay that for you.

According to the platform, donors cover project fees about 95% of the time, so you get to keep more of what you raise. GiveForward is very customer-focused. They even have personal coaches to help you every step of the way! Reviews for this platform are mostly positive, though there were some negative reviews by users who weren't as tech savvy. Customers like the simplicity of the platform, but some also had some concerns.

One user left a negative review saying, "I am very disappointed with Give Forward and their process of payment and lack of customer service. WePay was very helpful in getting the funds to our bank account, but I got little to no help from Give Forward. Their customer service was very rude and matter of fact and just told me to speak to We Pay for help. No follow up, no concern about not funding the bank account which was rejected 3 times."

However, another user reported on TrustPilot that, "GiveForward turned out to be a remarkable choice for our fundraiser. They were easy to use, supportive throughout the process, and even though I had an issue that resulted from (my own) user error, they made it right for me."

GiveForward is one of the leaders in this space and has done a great job helping personal fundraisers. Given the responsiveness of the team on TrustPilot, it seems like the company will be taking some of the negative critiques into consideration.

#5: Generosity

Generosity is a personal fundraising platform run by Indiegogo. Unlike the last two platforms we've looked at, there are no platform fees for launching a Generosity campaign, just a 3% + 30 cent transaction fee per donation. Instead, the platform relies on optional donations from donors to operate, helping project creators keep more of what they raise.

It only takes a few minutes to set up a Generosity page, and their Customer Happiness Team is there to answer any questions throughout the process. Reviews for their service seem to be mixed though, and they aren't easy to find since Generosity used to be (for a short time) Indiegogo Life. Some reviews complain about issues with customer service and users only receiving funds two weeks after their campaign ended.

For example, one user reported on BestCompany that "Generosity by Indiegogo really SUCKS! My donations have been held for over 60 days now. They keep passing me from department to department to no avail. I am so happy I moved my fundraiser to Go Fund Me which is working beautifully. This crowdfunding platform is just not worth it!"

However, the website also has numerous examples of successful campaigns like the fund to give Karen -The bus monitor- H Klein A Vacation. The 68-year-old bus monitor named Karen Klein was verbally harassed by middle schoolers on the way home from Athena Middle School. This campaign raised $703,168 in one month from 32,251 people.

As another example, a campaign raised money for the tragic murders of Warrant Officer Patrice Vincent & Corporal Nathan Cirillo. The campaign raised $393,450 CAD by 3,452 people in 7 days.

Like with the other platforms mentioned in this list, there are positives and negatives that come with Generosity.

#6: CrowdRise

Apparently if you're a fast typer it only takes 42 seconds create a fundraising website on CrowdRise! They offer flexible funding, fast access to funds, with customer service that can be reached via social media, email or live chat (it works, I tried it). In my experience, more organizations and non-profits tend to use CrowdRise, but it can also be used for personal expenses.

CrowdRise has two plan options: a free-to-launch plan that takes a 5% fee (including transaction fees) per donation, and a $50/month plan that has a 3% fee per donation but includes a lot of extra features (like a dedicated account manager and private training session). This is another platform where donors also have the option of paying fees for you, but if they don't, CrowdRise guarantees that they won't be higher than 3% - 5%. Most reviews of CrowdRise are great, many of them raving about the quality of their customer service. However, there are some negative reviews, mainly about the website's fee structure.

One positive review on SiteJabber reads, "My friend and I started a CrowdRise page to help find a cure for her daughters illness. We are not computer savvy and this was our first time at this kind of stuff--and we messed it up big time. Not only on the CrowdRise site but on the WePay site. Falco was able to understand the problem and took the initiative to coordinate with WePay to get things sorted out--all the while maintaining a sense of humor and with a great deal of patience. I would recommend to his boss that he gets some recognition/reward for his commitment to great customer service! Lisa Jones"

A negative review highlights that, "The fees associated with this organization made me not want to contribute. I did this one time but will not do it again. Shameful!"

Another reads, "I committed some money to a very good cause (a child's dangerous heath condition) via this bad service, and paid a most obnoxious fee ($13.00) to make the donation. I had to commit as a matter of honor and duty to my family, but I find this sort of venture reprehensible. I am also struck by the irony, the only amusing aspect of this experience,of Ed Norton and his liberal sorts making a fortune off the group efforts, need, and pain of others with this incredibly capitalistic enterprise."

As you know, I've mentioned other platforms that allow users to donate to the website. As the campaign creator, it's best to clear this up in your messaging if you don't want your donors to be surprised when they end up giving more than they expected. I'll talk more about this in chapter 4 and other outreach mistakes.

#7: Fundly

The Fundly crowdfunding platform has helped over 100,000 donation websites raise more than $300 million since they launched in 2009! Fundly was acquired by NonProfitEasy in

2015. Fundly is optimized to be viewed and managed on a range of mobile devices with Fundly's free mobile app. Mobile optimization is a priority for a lot of crowdfunders. This way you can access the platform from just about anywhere, at any time. Fundly also offers flexible funding and quick fund withdrawal.

Starting a campaign on Fundly is free. They charge a platform fee of 4.9% of funds raised, and there is a credit card processing fee of 2.9% + 30¢ per transaction (varies for international projects). The more you raise, the more the platform fee will drop.

I wasn't able to find any negative reviews about Fundly. But, there are a lot of campaigns that have raised funds. At the time of writing, A Ray of Hope is a live Fundly campaign that has raised over $178,000+ from 90+ donors. The campaign's creator, Lee Morgan, is trying to raise "raising $280,000 to build the first educational and therapy center for children with special needs in Tiruvannamalai, India!"

#8: Plumfund

Plumfund is a newer personal crowdfunding website that gives you the option to raise money for a variety of causes including baby showers, birthdays, travel, weddings, and more. Believe it or not, the site is free for fundraisers and donors, though you'll have to cover the payment processing fees.

Plumfund is a companion website to the team's other established platform, HoneyFund, which is a honeymoon registry and cash wedding gift registry. I wasn't able to find any online reviews for Plumfund, as their still a young platform.

Conclusion – Which is Best?

Deciding which platform is best for you depends a lot on the type of campaign you are running, the type of fee structure that you are comfortable with, and the level of customer support that you'll need. I recommend taking a thorough look at each website before making your decision.

Once you decide what platform you are going to use, you can start thinking about the different elements of your campaign and get ready to put together your fundraising page! This is what I'll be covering next.

Chapter 3: Creating a Great Campaign

A great crowdfunding campaign is easy to spot. It's successfully raised money! But, how do you actually put one together? How do you actually get donors to give money to your campaign? I'm going to be covering that and more in this chapter on how to put together your personal crowdfunding campaign.

There are a lot of advantages to investing in real estate under the JOBS Act crowdfunding exemptions. For example, you can now invest smaller amounts in a real estate opportunity alongside other investors (think $5,000), rather than taking on a huge investment by yourself. Also, you can easily create a well-diversified investment portfolio. REC has certainly made this asset class more accessible for accredited investors. Soon, unaccredited investors will also be able to take part in REC deals.

#1: Create a high quality pitch or "ask"

For some reason, we think that the online world is different from the physical world that we live in each day. It's not. Just like in person, your appearance matters online. The best way to turn off a potential donor from giving money to your personal crowdfunding campaign is with spelling errors, low quality images, poorly written paragraphs, and a superficial reason that explains why you're trying to raise money.

One way to cut down on spelling errors, awkward grammar, and run-on sentences is to read your pitch out loud! No, I don't mean to yourself. I mean read it out loud. Your writing voice should be no different than your speaking voice. Writing is just another form of communication and your goal in composing a personal crowdfunding pitch should be to communicate your need to another human being. There's no worse way to keep yourself at a distance than to use stilted language or incorrect grammar.

Another way to capture attention is with headlines and bolded or italicized words. There's a reason that textbooks, newspaper articles, blogs, and magazines use headlines to separate blocks of text. It makes it much easier to scan through the content and pick out sections that are relevant to you. It seems like a no-brainer, but many campaigns I see read like long essays. Make it easy for people to go through the elements of the pitch with descriptive and eye-catching titles so that they don't look at long blocks of text and close the browser window. Also, you might not think it, but when people are scanning an article or pitch, their eyes really do gravitate towards bolded words, links, and italics. Use these tools to convey tone or emotion with your pitch.

In addition, writing, pictures, and a video that evokes emotion is at the cornerstone of great storytelling. These elements are crucial for getting a visitor that's looking at your campaign page to connect with you and your cause. I'll cover the basics of storytelling in another point, but for now, you should start to think about ways that you can make your need or the reason that you're raising money more "real" or "concrete."

Finally, there is no bigger turn off than someone coming to your campaign page, thinking that you're really in need and genuinely asking something of them, only to find that the cause or whatever it is that you're raising money for is superficial and greedy. Crowdfunding should always be a last resort or, if you're offering interesting "perks" and "rewards," a way to involve your supporters in your mission. If you're unaware, perks or rewards are a way of thanking your donors for supporting your campaign. In exchange for giving money to your fundraiser, they'll get access to physical or digital rewards, like a t-shirt, a shout out on Facebook, or a handwritten letter. If you take anything away from this paragraph it should be that, crowdfunding is not an excuse to be lazy. It's only to be used for legitimate needs when there is no other option.

#2: Anticipate objections you'll receive

Take a second to put yourself in the shoes of a donor. This could be a friend, a member of your church group, or a friend of a friend. What would they think when they come across your crowdfunding campaign?

Write down all of the objections that you might receive to this fundraiser. Maybe they won't think the need is genuine. Maybe they can't afford to give. Maybe they don't understand why this cause is important? Write it down. The goal with your campaign page is to turn lurkers into donors. One way you'll do that is to anticipate the objections that are going to come up and to address them with your text or video.

Let's say that you're trying to raise money for college or education-related expenses. Have you exhausted all other options? Crowdfunding your education should not be the go-to or primary method of financing your entire university or post-university education. Traditional methods like loans, work-study, and part-time jobs are still the best way to put yourself through a degree program. Unfortunately, taking on debt and/or working while attending classes is what is required to earn a degree and benefit from a higher future income. You need to address this in your campaign.

Also, it's important to think about the value your future career will bring to society. One of the largest sources of pledges for donation-based crowdfunding campaigns is from the creator's social network and local community. I believe this is the case because these groups are most likely to benefit from pledging money to the campaign (whether emotionally, or practically). If you're going to be raising money to fund an education that provides little value to society, then it will be harder to convince backers that the investment is worthwhile. However, if you are attempting to prepare for a degree as a doctor in a low-income community that is lacking in access to healthcare, you will have an easier time convincing backers that the endeavor is worthwhile. Again, you must anticipate any pushback that you might receive.

Okay, now let's change up the example a little. Maybe you're trying to raise money for travel expenses. While it's tempting to create a crowdfunding page in an afternoon, throw it up in the evening, and hope that by the time you wake up in the morning, you'll have raised a bunch of money from amazing supporters, that just doesn't happen.

Instead, you need to first think about why people would want to support your journey and what value you can bring them in exchange for their hard earned cash. Let's say that you are raising money for a mission trip to El Salvador, a poor Latin American country, where you will be teaching children, exposing them to good role models, and attempting to encourage them to pursue peaceful behaviors, rather than a life of gang-violence and drugs.

Instead of asking people to give you money so that you can pay for the expenses to volunteer, you should think about why they would want to support your cause. If they are a part of your religious organization, how are you forwarding that org's mission and goals? How are you bringing your religions values to other parts of the world? Why will this experience make you a better person and more inclined to have a larger positive impact when you return? Instead of supporting a larger charity, members of your church could receive real-time photo and video updates from you throughout your travels. They could directly see how their money is making an impact.

In addition, it's likely that members of an organization tend to look to leaders in that community for advice and guidance. If you are able to convince a higher up member that your cause is worthy, then others who might be skeptical of the technology or mission may be more willing to listen to your proposal and support it!

But, what if you're trying to raise money for a "fun" trip, like a honeymoon destination? Guess what? There are many people out there that have successfully crowdfunded their honeymoon using sites like HoneyFund! I think these types of trips are a bit more difficult to gather support for. One way to deal with objections that you'll get is that if the "for fun" trip is related to a major life event like a wedding or a graduation, rather than asking for gifts or other showings of congratulations, you could ask people to consider pledging to your crowdfunding campaign.

For example, a Wallstreet Journal Article reported that "Gerald and Rachel Monaco, a San Francisco couple, decided to ask their wedding guests for $9,000 for a honeymoon to Finland." Although the couple only raised $1,900, they were able to make the trip through a combination of the campaign, monetary gifts not given through the crowdfunding platform, and their own savings. You could also consider coming up with some interesting rewards or perks for contributors, like bringing home gifts from abroad or hosting a dinner when you get back where you cook authentic cuisine.

#3: Tell a story, include personal facts, and invite donors into your world.

Stories are everywhere. They're found in books, movies, and video games, but did you know that stories are also a great way to create a memorable impression?

Think about some of your favorite commercials.

Remember the 2015 Budweiser Super Bowl Commercial? It's about a puppy and a horse who are best buds and always have each other's backs (it's adorable). They packed so much emotion into this simple commercial.

A compelling story is memorable and relatable. It makes an audience feel a certain way.

By building a story into your fundraiser's pitch, you'll stand out as an actual human being who donors can relate to and feel empathy for. Empathy is extremely important when soliciting donations. When a member of your social network is able to connect with how you're feeling or what you went through, they are far more likely to make a donation and help your cause. Also, by including well-known personal facts in your story or campaign pitch, you'll give visitors a chance to re-connect with you. These facts might even conjure up memories that they've shared with you.

There are seven basic plot types. You might not realize it, but most stories follow a repeatable format. In fact, after studying Jungian psychology and the archetypes that have recurred throughout human history, Christopher Booker created a list of seven basic stories that can be found around the world. He published these in his 2006 book, The Seven Basic Plots: Why We Tell Stories.

When you are creating your pitch video or overall campaign message, keep these basic plot types in mind and see if any of them fit well with your pitch.

1. Overcoming the Monster. In this type of story, the main character must defeat an evil force to save himself or his family. That evil force could be tangible or intangible.

2. Rebirth. When a protagonist must change his or her ways after a pivotal event, they are reborn into a better person. The topic of rebirth can be used in a wide variety of ways for different types of crowdfunding campaigns.

3. Quest. When embarking on a quest, a main character or group of characters have one object of desire and must overcome obstacles in order to attain it. Quests are very common in traditional storytelling and instantly command attention. You

might be on a quest to find the perfect product to solve a problem, or to better the world in some specific way.

4. Journey and Return. Journey and return stories (like the lost puppy in the Budweiser commercial) are classics that many people can relate to. Often times, throughout the journey, the main character must fight through a bunch of forces that threaten their return. When they do return, they come back with loads of experience and a great story.

5. Rags to Riches. Everyone loves rags to riches stories because they give us hope that our own circumstances can always change for the better. In a typical rags to riches story, a protagonist acquires some form of wealth, only to experience new found issues, which must be corrected for him to grow as a person. I'll admit, it's harder to implement this type of story into a personal crowdfunding campaign. But, I wanted to include it in case it sparked any ideas!

6. Tragedy. A tragedy follows a protagonist's downfall. Think Breaking Bad or Scarface. You could use this archetype to build empathy for a cause-related campaign. Many medical fundraisers or disaster relief funds employ this type of story, (like the case of a seriously injured puppy).

7. Comedy. I'm sure you know this genre. But don't forget, even the best comedies include conflict in their story. There are many ways that comedy can be used to tell a story about a crowdfunding campaign. Despite raising money for a horrible issue, you could add humor and personality to the story to remind donors of why they love you and your underlying spirit, despite the difficult circumstances.

Sometimes it seems like the stories around us (in movies, TV shows and books) were made for us. They touch us on a deep level and make us think even after they are over. Many individuals in the marketing industry have learned to harness that storytelling power and use it to their advantage. When you are planning your crowdfunding campaign, think of ways that you can incorporate storytelling. It can help you communicate a complicated message in a way that potential donors might understand more.

At the end of the day, you're using all of these techniques to make donors FEEL something when they come to your campaign page. A great personal crowdfunding campaign evokes emotions, which prompts visitors to open their wallet and donate. In the next chapter, I'll talk about a few common mistakes that can cost you donations.

Chapter 4: Outreach Mistakes (What not to do)

More often than not, success in the personal crowdfunding arena comes from avoiding costly mistakes rather than using some kind of secret outreach technique. The reason I say that is because many of the mistakes that I'm about to mention can turn off donors, stop donors from giving money once they're on your campaign page, or prevent them from paying attention to you on various social media outlets.

You're trying to build, what in marketing terms, we call a "sales funnel." Let's say that you post this message on Facebook, "Please, please, please give me money to help me pay bills __link__." If 100 people view this update about your crowdfunding campaign on social media, 5 of those 100 check it out, and 1 person gives, you have a conversion problem.

The way you solve this problem is to figure out where in the process your numbers are off. Maybe you try some different messaging like, "I'm SO thankful for the 25 people who are helping me in this difficult time, especially ____, ____, and ____. Every dollar counts and $25 will get you a free batch of my delicious homemade cookies." Let's say of those 100 people that view this update, 50 people check it out and 10 contributes to the fundraiser. You've identified that the initial messaging you sent was coming off as "begging" or "pleading" and people didn't like that. Your new messaging worked better!

Obviously, you're not a marketing expert and you don't have the time to keep running tests like this to figure out the best practices for a fundraising campaign. That's why I've put together these common outreach mistakes. Avoid them at all costs!

#1: Don't spam your link on social media or on the web

If you go on my blog, CrowdCrux.com, or my YouTube channel, YouTube.com/CrowdCrux, you'll see hundreds, in some cases thousands of people spamming the link to their personal crowdfunding campaign. Here are three examples:

"Anything will help ____link_____."

"Please donate to _____link_____."

"____link____"

Yes, some of these pleads or spammy posts just have the link to the individuals' personal crowdfunding campaign. This is not an effective strategy, and you're simply wasting time. As I outlined in Chapter 1, strangers are not very likely to go to your campaign, particularly if you're spamming your link all over the web.

This rule also applies to your own social network. Don't just send update after update or tweet after tweet asking for money, linking to your campaign, and pleading your friends to help (I'll get more into that in the next point). Not only will you come off as desperate, but you'll alienate any supporters that you COULD have attracted.

As strict as I am about this rule, I am 100% empathetic. I understand why people do it. It's really because they don't know what else to do, are desperate, and they're panicking because they haven't received any donations. I'm not here to criticize your fundraising need. I'm here to show the effective way of getting attention and donations for it.

#2: Don't plead, beg, or show desperation

This applies mainly to crowdfunding campaigns related to medical, emergency, or personal expenses. The reason I highlight this mistake is because desperation is the number one turnoff in all areas of life. It will turn people off from wanting to be your friend, date you, or in this case, give money to your fundraising campaign.

The reason that desperation has this effect is because it's absolutely clear that you're focused on the transaction. You're only thinking about what you want. You have no confidence in your own value or self-worth. You come off as having no self-respect. People don't want to be associated with this type of energy or the feelings of guilt and awkwardness that this energy creates.

You also don't have any social proof. By that, I mean that if you're begging, it's unlikely that many people have helped you or taken a second to help you. Therefore, anyone who was on the fence about helping you is more likely to scroll past the message in their newsfeed. If they saw that 10 of your mutual friends had given to your campaign, they'd be more likely to stop and give to your fundraiser, because it's the socially acceptable thing to do. Here's social proof explained:

"Social proof is a type of conformity. When a person is in a situation where they are unsure of the correct way to behave, they will often look to others for cues concerning the correct behavior."

I know that what I just said in the last two paragraphs sounds harsh. But, it's human nature.

#3: Don't just post on Facebook or other channels and ASSUME your messages are seen.

Due to Facebook algorithm changes and the sheer volume of content on social media, it's highly unlikely that every one of your friends is going to see your status update or message when you share it. Therefore, direct outreach is crucial for getting donations. You have to be willing to call, text, message, and talk to your family, friends, and local network.

Any time that you are trying to engage in broad messaging or "talk to a group," it's less likely that you'll get donations. Although group messaging does have its place, the most reliable way that you're going to get contributions to your fundraiser is to message each person on an individual basis. When you take the time to personally message a friend, it makes them feel valued, respected, and special. If you're just posting the message on Facebook, they could scroll past, because they assume that other friends that you have will donate to the campaign. Direct outreach will also give you the opportunity to handle objections or worries that donors might have about contributing money to your campaign.

#4: Failure to share your campaign

I don't even think I need to make this point, but I do get questions about it, so I'll include it. You MUST share your personal crowdfunding campaign with your social network. This is the only way that you're going to get funds.

In chapter 1, we covered the myth that personal fundraisers will receive donations from strangers. They won't! You have to be willing to talk about your campaign, explain it, and share it with your friends, family, and local community. If you're not willing to do that out of embarrassment or fear of what people will think, you have two options. First, you could combat these fears, do some internal work, and push through them. Second, you could quite simply not do a personal crowdfunding campaign. There are other options out there to raise funds. I'll be talking about one option in chapter 6.

But, there is hope out there for you if you have a very dedicated friend or group of friends that are willing to help you with this campaign. They could put up the personal fundraiser FOR you and raise money on your behalf. This is how many successful fundraisers have started. It adds social proof to the campaign, makes it come off as less self-indulgent, and it's more socially acceptable.

#5: Skimping on your campaign page

The last mistake that I've seen time and time again by individuals trying to raise money with crowdfunding is failing to put themselves in the shoes of those people viewing the campaign.

Just because you know that this need is genuine, that you're a good person, and that you've contributed a lot to your friends and local community doesn't mean that other people will make that connection. You really have to spell it out for them. You have to tell your story. You're going to be doing this with your campaign text, images, and video. Don't be afraid to toot your own horn, because no one else is going to!

I'd recommend showing your campaign page to one or two of your friends and getting their honest feedback. What parts seem confusing? What questions do they have? How do you come off? I admit, it's really hard to get outside of your head and view your fundraising page with a fresh set of eyes. But, it's going to pay huge dividends.

These are some of the mistakes that you should avoid when putting together your campaign page. But, the real secret sauce of crowdfunding comes when you have to market your campaign page. That's what I'm going to cover next, along with some specific tactics and techniques that you can use to get more donations.

Chapter 5: Marketing Your Campaign

Whenever I speak with personal crowdfunding campaigners, they dread the idea of marketing their campaign. A lot of excuses will come up, like "I don't have the time," or "I don't want to bug people." Unfortunately, if you want to get funds, you're going to have to market your campaign. If you aren't willing to market your fundraiser, then you can check out chapter 6, which talks about an alternative to personal crowdfunding. I'll be covering marketing in specific verticals, like fundraisers for weddings and education-related costs at the end of this section.

Step #1: Re-establish old relationships

I like to think of crowdfunding as relationship-building at scale. Basically, you're "cashing in" on all of the amazing value that you've brought into the lives of your friends, family, and social network. These are people who know, like, and trust you. But, even though you might have positively impacted other people, you still have to re-establish your relationship with them before launching a campaign!

If you haven't talked with some college friends for several years or rarely speak to your childhood friends, then now is a good time to chat them up! You don't want to be asking them to donate to your campaign right off the bat. First, you want to become a part of their lives again. Simply by picking up the phone and having a conversation a month or two before the launch of your fundraiser can make it that much easier to tell them about it when it's time.

Remember that the biggest turn-offs in crowdfunding or friendship building are neediness and desperation. If you start a dialogue before you need something from another person by making jokes, grabbing a beer after work, or inviting them out to lunch, you'll come off as less needy when you do mention the campaign at a future date.

Step #2: Prime your network

Priming your network is all about warming up your friends, family, and acquaintances to your need and the concept of crowdfunding. First, you're going to start with your closest friends.

As you're introducing the concept of crowdfunding, you'll likely encounter many of the objections that you'll face among your other friends and family members. These could include comments like, "Is it safe to give this site my credit card" or "I don't understand…" You'll have a chance to address these objections with your closest connections and then address them with other people that you introduce to the campaign, either in your emails, Facebook messages, or on the actual campaign page.

You want to get the core group of your closest friends to give to your campaign on the first day that you announce your fundraiser. If possible, you could even ask these friends to run the campaign on your behalf.

When you have people giving on the first day, it gives the campaign some social proof, which we discussed in chapter 4. It will also give you an excuse to share your campaign, because you'll be publicly thanking these early donors. Finally, it will establish an average giving level, whether that's $25 or $50, which will impact how much other people who come to your page decide to give.

Step #3: Gather email addresses

You're going to be announcing the launch of your online fundraiser on the social media platform's that you're a part of, like Instagram, Facebook, Twitter, and SnapChat. But, don't neglect email, which still is one of the top source of pledges for most crowdfunding campaigns.

At the time of writing, you can export all of the email addresses of your Facebook email list using Yahoo Mail's export feature. You use a free email list managing software like MailChimp (free up to 2,000 subscribers) to see who opens the email blasts that you send out and which links they click. If you host a fundraising event or party, you could also ask for email addresses at this event. Finally, you could ask people to specifically subscribe to your newsletter for an important update about your life. If you're not seeing any subscribers to this list, you could individually message each friend on Facebook or via text message and ask them for their email address. Why? Because of the Facebook algorithm, not everyone is going to see status updates that you post. However most of your friends will see your emails and open them if they see that they're coming from you.

Step #4: Techniques to prompt giving

It's your job to get people to take action. Before we talk about ways to do that, let's get inside the head of donors. How do donors want to feel when they give money to a campaign? They want to feel:

1. Appreciated. Like you are personally thankful for their contribution. No one wants to feel like a cog in a machine or one face among many. We all want to feel special. That's why handwritten thank yous and letters are still so effective at creating positive feelings. Doesn't it feel good when someone calls you out by name and thanks you among a group of friends or even strangers? It increases your perceived value in that setting, which makes you feel good.

2. Like they're a good person. If I gave to a charity or cause and knew for a fact that money fed 10 children in Africa, I'd feel good

about myself. By making the impact of someone's funds tangible, you're more likely to elicit this type of feeling.

3. That they're part of a group. Human beings have a natural desire to do what is socially expected and to avoid areas or activities that are deemed to be socially odd. If you look in the window of a restaurant and see that there's no one there, you're less likely to eat there. You don't want people to feel weird, odd, or like they're alone when giving to your campaign. You want them to feel like they're part of a big group of friends and supporters who are contributing (yes, social pressure works).

The reason that I bring up these feelings is that personal crowdfunding is all about turning lurkers into supporters and advocates. You're going to have people who know that you're running a fundraiser, but for whatever reason, haven't given to it. The more that you focus on bringing out the above feelings in them, the more likely they are to give. In addition, the more you use the techniques that we talked about previously, like using images and storytelling, the more likely visitors will empathize with your need or situation.

If you assembled a core group of friends who are advocates and that are going to help with the fundraiser, you can leverage their social clout along the way by getting them to like the update statuses that you post, leave comments, or like the status of anyone who publicly commits to giving to your campaign.

In a Step-By-Step Fundraising article, non-profit management and fundraising expert Sandra Sims lists the top five reasons why people give to charitable causes:

• Personal experiences;

• They want to make a difference;

• They want to do something active about a problem or take a stand on a particular issue;

- They are motivated by personal recognition and benefits;
- Giving is good thing to do.

Another article in Fundraising123 backs up many of these top motivations for donating to charity or causes.

- Someone I know asked me to give, and I wanted to help them.
- I felt emotionally moved by someone's story
- I want to feel I'm not powerless in the face of need and can help (this is especially true during disasters)
- I want to feel I'm changing someone's life
- I feel a sense of closeness to a community or group

Many of these motivations have to do with emotions. When you're pitching your campaign, consider which emotions you are catering to in your potential donor demographic. Is this an opportunity to change someone's life, or does your story have strong emotional appeal? How can you highlight people that do donate, to give them that feeling of "recognition"?

Another way to prompt giving is to underscore the time sensitive nature of the campaign. If you're running a personal fundraiser that will end at a specific date, you can use this countdown to create a sense of urgency. With so many things going on in our lives, a new online fundraiser ranks low on the list of priorities. Your goal should be to bring it from priority #10 on someone's list to #3, or at the very least, in the top 5. Since their donation will only help up until a specific date, they're going to need to make your fundraiser a priority if they want to help out.

Ultimately, you want to take advantage of every excuse to share or talk about your campaign, whether it's celebrating milestones, asking people to push you over the edge if you're close to a round number, or thanking people publicly.

Fundraising for Weddings

You can use crowdfunding to raise money for just about anything, including your wedding. It's not unheard of for couples to raise modest amounts of money to help pay for their big day or their honeymoon.

For example, Katherine Donahue recently raised $3,248 on Generosity for her and her husband's honeymoon fund after getting married at City Hall in NYC.

With traditional weddings becoming less common, is crowdfunding your wedding (or some aspect of it) an acceptable thing to do?

Remember, strangers aren't going to give money to your crowdfunding campaign. Your friends, their friends, and your family are going to be contributing to your fundraising campaign.

You're going to have to announce the campaign to your friends. Many couples have embraced this concept, creating an online honey moon registry with HoneyFund (couples have raised $330,715,070), or used a popular crowdfunding site like GoFundMe.

For example, Jamie & Emma raised £7,545 on GoFundMe to help finance their wedding. Also, Maria & Dexter raised $3,705 on GoFundMe.

In some cases, using crowdfunding for your wedding can work well. More people are familiar with crowdfunding now, especially young adults, and it can save them the effort of going out and buying a gift. Plus, friends and family get to contribute in a way that is really meaningful to the couple.

At the same time, if the campaign isn't introduced in the right way to friends, family, and guests, it can come off as "begging" "selfish" or "rude."

It's your job to break the news to your guests, explain to them how to think about the fundraiser, and do the "customer service" by answering questions.

Believe it or not, many people are launching wedding crowdfunding campaigns, and many of those campaigns raise $0. The majority of successful projects seem to raise about $2,000 to $5,000 from roughly 25 people.

Bottom line: Some people think that crowdfunding for weddings is inappropriate. If you decide to go down this route, follow the simple rules and guidelines that I'm about to share in this next section. While it's possible to do this well, crowdfunding your wedding the wrong way can come across as selfish, leaving you with no donations and little pride.

Tip #1: Best practices

If you and your significant other are going to be paying for your wedding alone, the costs can quickly spiral out of control. Many couples have been left with a choice: "Do we cancel our wedding and just go to city hall?" The other option is asking your guests for money to help fund the wedding, rather than having them give you gifts.

If you decide that crowdfunding is a good option for you, make your page as personal as possible. An adorable photo of the couple along with a good love story can really encourage people to donate.

Pages with generic pictures and short, improperly spelled pleas for help paying for your wedding won't be effective. You need to be genuine and reach out to people who you think will want to help (yes on a personal level). This includes asking people one-on-one and not just posting a link to your campaign page over and over on Facebook.

Some other things that you can do to make the process go smoothly are: being very thankful to all of your contributors, posting cute pictures of yourselves as a couple, posting updates on your planning and progress, and showing people what you will use the money on. You could share on your page that you need money to pay for a venue, catering, music, etc.

If you need to ask people to help pay for some of your wedding, don't plan something too extravagant. Sandy Malone, Owner of Sandy Malone Weddings & Events ranted about this in a blog post:

"In a couple of cases, [couples] were having destination weddings their parents couldn't afford to attend and they want somebody to pick up that tab for their parents ... Hold up, wait a minute! You're having a destination wedding, but your parents cannot afford to come? What were you thinking when you decided to have a destination wedding in the first place?"

You don't want to put all of the weight of paying for your dream wedding on your guests. The same goes for campaigns looking to raise thousands for a wedding dress. If you can't afford it, you may need to settle for something a little more in your price range. If possible, you should make sure that your guests don't feel obligated to contribute to your crowdfunding campaign, and are still welcome even if they can't donate.

Simple dos:

• Contact each guest personally to explain the campaign and answer questions

• Thank people publicly so people can see that others are donating and be reminded of the campaign.

• Use rich media (photos, video)

• Tell the story of your love relationship

- Evoke emotion

Simple don'ts:

- Have spelling errors, bad photos, or little text
- Fail to explain why you're doing this
- Post your campaign link everywhere
- Plead or beg
- Be unreasonable in your goal and planning

Tip #2: What platform should you choose?

If you want to go ahead and crowdfund your wedding, you do have a lot of options to choose from in terms of crowdfunding platforms. You could go with just about any personal crowdfunding platform, but know that there are also some that deal specifically with weddings and honeymoons.

Honeyfund is one example where thousands of couples have successfully raised money to honeymoon in destinations including the Hawaiian Islands, France, Italy, Greece, and more! They also have options like retail registries and fundraisers where guests can donate to a charity of your choice rather than buy a gift.

Also, I would recommend looking into is Tilt (formerly Crowdtilt). The reason I suggest this over other crowdfunding platforms is that Tilt has a 91% success rate, which is much higher than some other platforms.

DepositAGift is another fundraising platform that allows you to customize the look and feel of your campaign page. I'd recommend looking into them along with the free webinar that we did on charity and personal fundraising, which I'll be including at the end of this ebook as bonus.

Finally, you can always get a low interest personal loan to help pay for the wedding. There are a lot of websites where you can do this. Here is a list of the different sites that stand out (http://www.crowdcrux.com/peer-to-peer-lending-sites/). The great thing about getting a loan through one of these sites is you'll get the money quickly and get a better rate than using credit cards.

Ultimately, the platform you choose should depend on the cost, ease of use, customer service and reputation. No matter what platform you launch on, you're going to have to work to promote your project or you will have a very hard time reaching your goal. A good platform can help you succeed, but they won't bring your donations to you.

So, should you crowdfund your wedding? Ultimately, the decision depends a lot on your guest list and the amount of effort you're willing to put in. If most of your guests don't use the internet or are concerned with doing things the 'proper' way, maybe crowdfunding isn't right for you.

If you and your significant other have an amazing love story and want to get married, but can't afford to pay for everything yourselves, crowdfunding is an option. If your friends and family are familiar with crowdfunding and seem open to contributing to your wedding or honeymoon this way, then go for it!

Just be sure that you shower any contributors with thanks and show them how their contribution will make a big difference for your big day. A bit of appreciation goes a long way.

Fundraising for Travel Expenses

Ever since the launch of Trevolta, a crowdfunding site for trips, I've been getting questions about how to crowdfund travel expenses and finance journeys outside of the country. Whether you are a student and want to study abroad, a member of a church or religious organization and want to plan a mission trip, or simply want to explore the world, you can incorporate crowdfunding into your travel plans.

Keep in mind that Trevolta is not the only crowdfunding website for travel expenses. You can also make use of Indiegogo, GoFundMe, and Kickstarter (if the funds go towards a specific project).

Step #1: Get a Clear Vision of Why People Would Support Your Journey.

While it's tempting to create a crowdfunding page in an afternoon, throw it up in the evening, and hope that by the time you wake up in the morning, you'll have raised a bunch of money from amazing supporters, that just doesn't happen.

Instead, you need to first think about why people would want to support your journey and what value you can bring them in exchange for their hard earned cash.

This analysis might not be as necessary if you are seeking a small amount, and are able to raise it from your close friends and family. These are the people who know and love you, and would support you no matter what. However, it will be critical if you are hoping for support outside of that small network.

For example, let's say that you are raising money for a mission trip to El Salvador, a poor Latin American country, where you will be teaching children, exposing them to good role models, and attempting to encourage them to pursue peaceful behaviors, rather than a life of gang-violence and drugs.

Rather than asking people to give you money so that you can pay for the expenses to volunteer, you should think about why they would want to support your cause. If they are a part of your religious organization, how are you forwarding that org's mission and goals? How are you bringing your religions values to other parts of the world? Why will this experience make you a better person and more inclined to have a larger positive impact when you return?

Instead of supporting a larger charity, members of your church could receive real-time photo and video updates from you throughout your travels. They could directly see how their money is making an impact.

In addition, it's likely that members of an organization tend to look to leaders in that community for advice and guidance. If you are able to convince a higher up member that your cause is worthy, then others who might be skeptical of the technology or mission may be more willing to listen to your proposal and support it!

Takeaway: You must brainstorm reasons why members of your network would feel compelled to support you and then use those points as a basis for a good pitch.

Step #2: Begin a Marketing Campaign That Involves Supporters

When I say a plan that "involves" your supporters, I mean coming up with a way to both spread awareness about your initiative, get feedback, and attract followers that care about your mission, cause, or what you're doing.

That might seem impossible, but if you take a second to think about it, there are countless travel bloggers, youtubers (vlogger), and podcasters who are able to use their talents to involve people in their life and make them care about a particular topic.

A few ideas to get started:

• Start a blog on wordpress, tumblr, or medium. Blog a minimum of 1 post per week leading up to the launch of your campaign. I would start as soon as possible (even if that's a year in advance). Be sure to set up an email capture form and prominently display your social media accounts so that people can keep up to track with your progress.

• Start a YouTube vlog or series that brings to attention to the reason for your trip. It will show people that you really are passionate about X and give them time to get used to the idea.

• Ask people to sign up to a weekly newsletter where you will be sharing updates leading up to the trip and throughout your travels.

• Host a party (you provide food or drinks) where the proceeds will be used to jumpstart your fundraising campaign. Make sure you get everyone in that party to share your initiative on their social media channels and subscribe to your newsletter. You could use a tool like Thunderclap to coordinate everyone's social media pledge or Aweber to host your email list.

What if the trip is "for fun?" I think these types of trips are a bit more difficult to gather support for. If the "for fun" trip is related to a major life event like a wedding or a graduation, rather than asking for gifts or other showings of congratulations, you could ask people to consider pledging to your crowdfunding campaign.

For example, a Wallstreet Journal Article reported that "Gerald and Rachel Monaco, a San Francisco couple, decided to ask their wedding guests for $9,000 for a honeymoon to Finland." Although the couple only raised $1,900, they were able to make the trip through a combination of the campaign, monetary gifts not given through the crowdfunding platform, and their own savings.

You could also consider coming up with some interesting rewards or perks for contributors, like bringing home gifts from abroad or hosting a dinner when you get back where you cook authentic cuisine.

Step #3: Make it Easy To Give

Crowdfunding has not yet gone mainstream. There are a lot of people in your network that won't know what crowdfunding is, whether or not it's safe, and how they can contribute to your campaign.

I'd recommend making a simple PDF or graphic overview that will explain what you are doing, what crowdfunding is, and how individuals can support you. Think dead simple and provide a step-by-step walkthrough for non-tech savvy users.

Don't forget to emphasize the time-sensitive nature of the crowdfunding campaign. Most people (myself included) have a bias towards laziness. If people read your email or see your Facebook post, they might want to support it, but simply forget or put it off, because it's not urgent. A specific deadline will help motivate your backers to get up off their butts and contribute while they can!

Ultimately, you know your network better than anyone else. By spending an hour thinking about some of the common FAQs that will come up, you will save yourself some headache and also ensure that more people will pledge, rather than ignoring your document or clicking off it because they don't fully understand the project.

Step #4: Use Social Proof and Shout-outs

With email, Twitter, Facebook, Pinterest, Instagram, LinkedIn, and Snapchat, it's easier than ever to get lost in the swarm of social feeds.

One way that you can improve the chances others will see and pay attention to your messages is to leverage the social proof behind your initiative. If your relatives see that other members of your family have already supported you, they will be more likely to pledge to your project. If you mention a friend on Facebook and thank them for pledging, they will probably like that post and possibly re-share it, making it more likely it will stand out in your friends' and their friends' feeds.

If you're planning your trip abroad with a particular organization or university, ask if you can use their logo on your fundraising page. It will raise the credibility of your crowdfunding campaign and if it's successful, it could be a good PR piece for that university, which could lead to further contributions or good press.

Step #5: Don't Give Up & Alternative Solutions

You can take all of these steps, read my other tips, and you still might not be successful initially or in the long run. Rather than being tempted to give up, you should evaluate the actions you are taking and their results. What is working? What isn't? This data will be different for every campaign.

There are sites like GoFundMe that will allow you to continually raise money over a long duration. You can use this time to figure out the best way to approach your network and communicate your project. Even if you are not successful, you will learn a tremendous amount from running a crowdfunding campaign.

Depending on your skill set, there are many other ways to finance your lifestyle while traveling abroad or during the time leading up to the trip. If you are volunteering while on the trip, you could consider some of these fundraising ideas. If you are studying abroad, you could use this opportunity to set up an online business or start a blog, which can help bring in some extra income.

Fundraising for Education

In the last year, we've seen a proliferation of education-centric crowdfunding campaigns and platforms. More and more debt-burdened students are turning to their local community and online groups to help finance their college or post-college education.

Can you really pay your tuition this way? Before you check out some of the tips below, consider the following ramifications.

Pre-Campaign Assessment:

1. Do you have any other options? Crowdfunding your education should not be the go-to or primary method of financing your entire university or post-university education. Traditional methods like loans, work-study, and part-time jobs are still the best way to put yourself through a degree program. Unfortunately, taking on debt and/or working while attending classes is what is required to earn a degree and benefit from a higher future income.

Before going to the lengths of preparing for a crowdfunding campaign, I'd recommend thinking hard about whether or not these other options are available to you.

2. What value will your future career bring? One of the largest sources of pledges for donation-based crowdfunding campaigns on platforms like GoFundMe is from the creator's social network and local community. I believe this is the case because these groups are most likely to benefit from pledging money to the campaign (whether emotionally, or practically).

If you're going to be raising money to fund an education that provides little value to society, then it will be harder to convince backers that the investment is worthwhile. However, if you are attempting to prepare for a degree as a doctor in a low-income community that is lacking in access to healthcare, you will have an easier time convincing backers that the endeavor is worthwhile.

3. Have you researched the subject of crowdfunding? Finally, before even getting into any tips or tricks for crowdfunding your education, I strongly recommend looking at other education

related campaigns that were successful and unsuccessful. What kind of outreach did they do? How much did they raise? Did they offer any tangible rewards to backers? Did they create a video?

All of this information will help you avoid making common mistakes, create a more engaging project, and ultimately increase your chances of success.

Crowdfunding Tip #1: Focus on the deliverables.

If possible, it will always be easier to crowdfund an education-related project than your entire college or university cost. This is because at the end of the day, your backers will have something tangible to show for their hard-earned investment in you. If you aren't able to put the funds towards a specific education project, then you need to be crystal clear about what backers will receive in exchange for pledging money to your campaign.

For example, in a TheNextWeb article, Vikas Lalwani described how he raised money that could be used for attending MakeGamesWithUs Summer Academy.

"I did a lot of research and realized that the basic difference between my campaign and any other crowdfunding campaigns on Crowdtilt or Kickstarter was that on these platforms, people trying to raise funds were promising an innovative product in return to all of their contributors.

This made me think about things that I can give in return to people who contribute to my cause. I pondered over ideas like teaching students, giving free access to my apps and others. But after a lot of brainstorming, I settled for this: make a full-fledged app for donors who contribute at least $1,000 towards my tuition."

In the above example, there is a tangible benefit for backing the student and helping them attend MakeGamesWithUs. You can have the opportunity to have your own app developed at a below-market price.

Crowdfunding Tip #2: Create a video.

According to Indiegogo's CEO, "If you have a video, you'll raise 114% more money on average than if you don't."

It's incredibly difficult to develop rapport online, and rapport is key when convincing strangers to support your endeavor or buy your products. "Building rapport is one of the most fundamental sales techniques. In sales, rapport is used to build relationships with others quickly and to gain their trust and confidence. It is a very powerful tool that veteran salespeople naturally employ, which allows them to close more deals with less effort." - Wikipedia.

The best way that you can develop rapport through a computer screen is with a video. The quickest way to destroy rapport online is with spelling mistakes, poorly formatted text, haphazard reward tiers, and a campaign page that looks like it was thrown together in a few minutes.

At the very least, if you cannot make a video (there is no real excuse that I can think of), then you must include photographs, testimonials, and list your achievements to build rapport. Treat it like a job interview.

Crowdfunding Tip #3: Create reward tiers.

I agree – it's difficult to come up with tangible and even intangible rewards for an education crowdfunding project. The idea is to show your appreciation and also involve your supporters in your educational journey. For example: If you want to become a lawyer and are raising money to complete your degree, why not offer a free legal consultation once you pass your required certification exams? If you want to become an app developer, you could offer to develop an iphone or android app for a below market rate.

Give people an incentive to support you, whether it's being willing to volunteer for the local community or a thoughtful and emotional thank you note.

Crowdfunding Tip #4: Reach out to your local network and local community.

I know you don't want to hear this, but your social network and local community is going to be the most likely set of backers for your education crowdfunding campaign. For example, in this Boston Globe article, Alexis-Brianna Felix shares how she raised over 5k for her education.

"Many donations came from friends Felix made at the Horace Mann School, a prestigious private college preparatory school in the affluent Riverdale section of the Bronx she was able to attend due to good grades and generous financial aid. Others came from alumni of the high school and BU, and from strangers."

Crowdfunding Tip #5: Set as low a goal as possible.

As we talked about in the last article, the average amount raised during a GoFundMe campaign is $1,126. 76% of users set a goal that is $1,000 or less. You may think that it would be nice to raise $150,000 and cover your entire tuition, but this is going to be near-impossible. Instead, focus on a small subset of your education costs (books?) or an education-related project that you would like to complete (study abroad, community service trip, etc).

Crowdfunding Tip #6: Explain what, why, where, how, and when.

Don't leave out the what, why, where, how and when. All of these elements should be included in your video pitch and campaign text. You need to treat your backers like investors and let them know exactly where their money will be going, why you need it, what it will be going towards, how you intend to accomplish your goals, and when they can expect their rewards or for you to accomplish your goals.

The key rule here is to pitch them with passion. Don't just list out why you need funds or where the money will go. Show them your passion for your educational endeavor. One backer in the campaign discussed in #4 said:

"We don't know each other, but I was touched by your courage, tenacity, and perseverance."

Crowdfunding Tip #7: Don't be humble.

You should treat the campaign almost like a job interview. What have you accomplished up to this point? Where do you see yourself going during university and after? Why can you accomplish your dreams? Don't forget to toot your own horn, because no one else will. Be confident in yourself!

Crowdfunding Tip #8: Be humble.

Sounds contradictory, but you also need to be humble. DO NOT BEG, but explain why any donations will change your life and how grateful you will be for any support.

Crowdfunding Tip #9: Hold yourself accountable.

How can you convince backers that any funds donated will have a real impact in your life and lead to real-world results? Any way that you can hold yourself accountable to your backers and keep the up to date with your progress will positively affect your chances of raising funds. I recommend starting a blog.

Crowdfunding Tip #10: Reach out to your heroes.

In the campaign described in #1, Vikas Lalwani reached out to his hero:

"I then started sending out emails asking for help and got contributions from highly respected people in the industry, including Reddit's Alexis Ohanian and a top investor from Andreessen Horowitz."

If you can describe how your hero has impacted your life thus far, it may increase the chances that he or she will respond to your email.

Bonus Content: Reward Ideas

The hallmark of great crowdfunding campaigns is a set of compelling rewards. The more GoFundMe campaigns I look at, the more I am convinced that both crowdfunding reward tiers and pitch videos are underutilized on the GoFundMe platform.

Just recently, Indiegogo reported that "Campaigns with a pitch video raise an average of 114% more than campaigns that don't."

I want to help you brainstorm rewards that you could incorporate into your personal crowdfunding project!

Volunteering Campaigns

When you are raising money for a volunteer initiative, you need to put your business cap on and think as a social entrepreneur.

Why would people support this volunteer initiative? What do they get out of it?

1. Sponsorships for Businesses. Corporate responsibility is a growing sector and is becoming increasingly important, as brands strive to stay relevant on social media networks.

By incorporating sponsorship tiers into your campaign, you can give companies the opportunity to support your volunteering initiative, while also helping them gain brand awareness in a new demographic. In addition, it's a great way they can show their stakeholders that they are giving back to the community, which is always a good PR story.

2. Images, Videos, and Thank You Cards. Sharing images and videos of your volunteering experience via a blog or other publishing platform is a great way to thank backers for supporting your initiative. In addition, it's content that businesses in your sponsorship tier can share on social media to demonstrate how they are giving back.

If your work deals with an underprivileged demographic, you could also have these individuals share their stories via thank you cards or videos to showcase how you are making a difference in their lives. You should use images, video, and other types of content to transfer the emotions you feel when volunteering (happiness/satisfaction) to your backers.

3. 1-for-1 Promotion. Although not specifically a reward tier, one way that you could rally support for a volunteering initiative is to approach local businesses about a 1-for-1 promotion.

As an example, a local business might agree to donate $5 to your campaign for every customer you bring to their pizza shop in the next week. You would use flyers or handouts to track which customers the business received from your promotional efforts. Your local community could enjoy food and their hard-earned money would have the added side effect of benefiting a cause!

4. Accountability and Impact Measurements. You might not think of it this way, but donating money is really an investment. When you give money to the Red Cross or a Hurricane Relief Fund, you are expecting that money to be put to work and make change. You value the change the funds make more than just having the money sit in your bank account.

The best way you can thank your backers is to hold yourself accountable and provide reports as to where the money is going, what impact it is making, and how your volunteer efforts are moving a cause forward. You could do this through reports or blog posts.

Education Fundraising Campaigns

Personally, I think education fundraising campaigns are the hardest type of campaign to raise funds for on personal crowdfunding sites.

Other young adults and adults are also going through the expensive university system. They are working at part-time jobs, going to class, taking out loans, and not getting much sleep. That's the price of becoming educated so that you can have a higher earning power in the future.

Though you may receive some charity donations from your social network, I first urge you to think whether or not you need funds for your education campaign, or if it would "just be nice." If it's the latter, don't do it.

5. Work Pro Bono or Volunteer. Using the skills you learn from your education to date and with your new education, you could work pro bono for non-profits and underprivileged demographics in the area. This could include teaching senior citizens how to use laptops to teaching a non-profit how to use social media. You could also agree to give back to the community by volunteering your time and labor.

6. Intern. If you could find a local company or entrepreneur to sponsor a portion of your education, you could agree to work for them as an unpaid intern (likely menial tasks, but any small business would welcome the extra hands). You could also agree to help promote their products or services on campus as a on-campus-representative.

Medical Costs & Emergency Campaigns

From my research, the majority of donations towards medical cost/emergency campaigns come from an individual's local network and local community. Yes, there are places like Reddit's charity section that you can use to gain stranger awareness or, if the story is compelling, there are instances where you can gain support through news stories.

I would strive to use your rewards to show appreciation for your donations that go beyond just a simple "thank you" note.

7. Host a get-together. Have you ever heard of fundraising dinners, where by "buying a plate" you are supporting a cause? You could take this same approach to raising funds from your local network or community. You may even be able to get donated foods from local restaurants for the event.

8. Show Your Thanks (literally). You could make a poster, Facebook cover image, or section of your blog/website that highlights all of the incredible supporters (names/faces) that were willing to help you through a tough time.

9. Group Hangout Thank You. If you are expecting to receive pledges from around the country, you could also provide access to a group google hangout to say thanks to all your supporters face-to-face, as well as get to know them a little.

I hope that some of these reward ideas sparked some thoughts! If you employ the marketing techniques we discussed in this section, you'll increase the chance of getting donors and hitting your fundraising goal! In the next section, I'll be covering an alternative to personal crowdfunding if you've decided that you don't want to use online fundraising.

Chapter 6: Alternatives to Personal Fundraising

Let's be honest, launching a personal crowdfunding campaign isn't for everyone. We've already gone over that you MUST be willing to let your family, friends, and social network know about your campaign. If you're not willing to do that, then this isn't the best route to go to raise money for personal costs.

However, there are other ways that you can get funding or money to help alleviate personal expenses or needs. I'd recommend looking into peer to peer lending.

What is peer to peer lending?

Most of us are familiar with credit cards, so let's start there. When you use your credit card, you are borrowing money from an institution with certain terms and conditions that you're expected to pay back at the end of the month.

If you don't pay the loan back, you'll be hit with an extremely high interest rate that will add to your overall debit. Unless you pay off your credit card quickly, you'll soon be amassing more and more credit card debt. This is similar to how banks work. When you get a loan from a bank, you're agreeing to pay back the funds on a payment schedule. If you fail to pay back all the funds at once, you'll incur interest charges, which adds to your total debt.

So how does P2P lending differ? One word: Software. A peer to peer lending platform functions as a marketplace with investors and borrowers. Their software will match investors up with your loan application. There is also no collateral. You're asking for an unsecured personal loan. Depending on your credit score, the term of the loan, and the type, you may experience a different APR (interest rate) for the loan you receive on the platform.

Because peer to peer lending platforms like Prosper and Lending Club use technology to connect lenders with borrowers, there is very little overhead and the websites can pass their savings on to you, facilitating lower interest rates.

What are the benefits of P2P Lending?

"Peer-to-peer lending for credit-worthy borrowers can provide more cost-effective personal loans, so that may be where peer-to-peer lending can play a meaningful role early on ... If they've got a good credit history, it's going to be a very competitive loan, so they effectively save themselves quite a lot of money." - Ratesetter chief executive Daniel Foggo.

As a borrower, there are a lot of benefits to this new lending model over the traditional banking or credit model. Here are a few:

- Online application means a quicker approval time
- Fixed repayment rate
- No collateral needed
- No prepayment penalties

Peer-to-peer lending is a new way to secure a loan for just about anything, with rates that are lower than traditional banks. You just list your loan on a p2p lending website and others around the world will fund it! Since these platforms are run mainly online, you save time and money by avoiding brick and mortar financial services.

What are the downsides?

"Remember, borrowers who take out P2P loans have the same obligations as they would after securing a bank loan. Defaulting on the loan will cause the P2P Web site to report the delinquency to the credit bureaus, which will damage the borrower's credit score." - Bankrate.com

Just like using a credit card or taking out a bank loan, you MUST pay back the loan granted from a P2P lending platform. This isn't free money, by any means. For someone who is already in need of funds, this can be a difficult reality, but you can take comfort in the fact that it's likely you'll be getting a better rate on the loan than if you were to use traditional credit cards.

Where can you get a loan with P2P lending?

There are two main websites that you can use to get a loan with peer to peer lending. These are Prosper and Lending Club.

Prosper is a US-Based peer-to-peer (p2p) lending platform that was founded in 2006. "Prosper is America's first peer-to-peer lending marketplace, with more than 2 million members and over $1,000,000,000 in funded loans." Using the website, you can borrow between $2,000 and $35,000 in the form of an unsecured personal loan.

Lending Club was founded in 2007 and is the largest peer to peer (p2p) lending platform in the US. "Fueled by the value we deliver, Lending Club has consistently grown at more than 100% per year each of the last few years. Since inception, we have facilitated more than $5 billion in loans, while paying more than $300 million in interest to investors. " What I like about Lending Club is their aggressive expansion into other areas of financing. For instance, they now offer patient financing loans for those that need help with medical bills.

Review of Prosper

Prosper allows borrowers to apply for loans between $2,000 and $35,000 at as little as 5.99% APR for their best borrowers. Loans are granted for a variety of expenses, including home improvement, business, vacation, medical/dental, and more.

To help shed light on this new area of crowdfunding, I decided to interview Jordan M. Mackey, the owner of real estate business Rnt2KC and a Prosper member since 2007.

How many loans have you taken out with Prosper?

Currently I've taken out three separate loans with Prosper. One of them has been paid off, while two are still current.

What is the average amount of time it takes to fund a loan on Prosper from your experience?

My third loan for $15,000 was funded in 7 HOURS!

Is there anything you dislike about the platform?

The community aspect was taken away, which was the initial reason why I signed up for the program. I loved the original capitalist nature of allowing borrowers to have their loan rates literally bid down by potential lenders. However, to handle their increased volume of loans, I believe they had to streamline the process and that feature ended up on the chopping block.

As mentioned above, I didn't get my third loans rate bid down. However, I did have it funded in 7 hours which in the residential banking world NEVER HAPPENS!

If you've interacted with staff from Prosper, how was their customer service?

Excellent, I've never had a single problem or issue with Prosper. On that same note any concern or questions I've had were answered in a very timely and professional manner!

Would you still recommend Prosper to someone who is looking for an alternative to traditional loans?

I'm a very loyal and loving fan of Prosper and their grassroots model. They have integrated a platform to put more power in the hands of small mom and pop businesses, as well as individual investors.

It's a very rare sight to see a company that can bring together a small-town Midwestern boy like myself and a multimillion dollar hedge fund together on the same platform.

Review of Lending Club

Lending Club groups loans into three different categories: personal, business and patient financing. It only takes minutes to apply for a personal loan on Lending Club, and you can get funded in as little as a few days. Borrowers that use Lending Club to consolidate debt or pay off high interest credit cards in one fixed monthly payment see rates reduced by an average of 33%.

There are no prepayment fees or penalties either – which gives you a chance to eliminate future interest payments and save more. Even better, getting a loan from Lending Club can actually boost your credit score.

"76% of borrowers experience a FICO score increase three months after obtaining their loan, with an average increase of 21 points!" Lending Club's 2014 – 2015 survey data shows.

The process is easy – just complete the fast application (which won't affect your credit score) and instantly review the loan offers you qualify for.

Lending Club's patient financing service offers doctors a way to easily provide their patience with better financing options so they can take more time to focus on their practice.

There are two different options for patient financing on Lending Club: Extended Plans and True No-Interest Plans. Extended Plans can be used to cover up to $50K in medical expenses with APRs starting at 3.99% and True-No Interest plans go up to $32K at 0% APR for up to 24 months. Lending Club currently offers specialized patient services in four areas: dentistry, fertility, hair and bariatric (weight loss surgery).

Overall, Lending Club has a 4.3 star rating on Credit Karma, with over 2000 total reviews. In October 2015, one loan holder shared:

"I have looked into consolidation loans before and nothing really worked or they seemed more complicated than I could deal with. This was so easy AND QUICK I'm still kind of spinning that the money is already in my account. WOW. Would recommend this to anyone."

Many people have left similar positive reviews of Lending Club, but one of the issues that people seem to have (that I've also seen with a few other P2P lending sites) is that people often get pre-approved fast but some are declined a few days later. That's what happened to this user who left a review on Pissed Consumer:

"Filled out app. Pre-approved instantly.

The initial process seemed easy. Submitted all information as requested. Received email that loan was fully funded and should have my loan soon. They even had access to my checking account.

I waited and waited. Finally received a call. They stated my numbers did not match their numbers exactly and they denied the loan. They did admit they were way behind ... Sounds too good to be true, it probably is. Would not recommend."

Lending Club does address the issue in an FAQ on their website. They note that:

"Common reasons for being declined for a loan after receiving a pre-approved offer are that an applicant's current outstanding debt is too high relative to their income or that changes have occurred in their credit report since pre-screening."

They also do mention that the application and funding process can take up to 14 days (or longer). I think that Lending Club could better manage this negative feedback by making some of this information a little more upfront. It's all there for those who look deeply enough, but a quick scan of their home page doesn't necessarily give borrowers the most realistic expectations – in most cases they are seeing the best case scenario.

Before you get a loan

Be sure to carefully think about the pros and the cons mentioned in this section. Again, this is not free money. There are costs associated with going this route, but if you're unwilling to share your personal fundraiser with friends and family, it is a viable alternative.

Chapter 7: Conclusion

Guess what?

You've reached the end of this ebook! Congratulations! BUT, I have one final bonus piece of content that I'd like to share with you.

Below, I'm going to link to a FREE video. It's a recorded online webinar that I co-hosted on the topic of Charity and Personal Fundraising.

It won't be available forever, so be sure to check it out.

---> [Free Charity and Personal Fundraising Webinar](https://www.youtube.com/watch?v=KJBvwdMH1lc) <---
(https://www.youtube.com/watch?v=KJBvwdMH1lc)

You don't have to enter your email or anything to access it.

But, would you mind leaving a positive review of this ebook on Amazon? It would mean so much to me!

I feel privileged that you took the time to read this ebook and I look forward to hearing about your crowdfunding success story!

- Sal

"Do your little bit of good where you are; it's those little bits of good put together that overwhelm the world." - Desmond Tutu

ABOUT THE AUTHOR

Salvador Briggman founded the popular blog, CrowdCrux, which has been cited by the New York Times, The Wallstreet Journal, CNN, and more. He helps entrepreneurs raise money on crowdfunding platforms like Kickstarter and Indiegogo. Last year, he helped nearly 400,000 individuals raise money from the crowd through his website, products, newsletter, and forum.

Made in the USA
Monee, IL
06 October 2020